Welcome

MW00389898

Guest Name: _____   Date Stayed: _____

Traveling From: _____   Weather: ☀ ☁ ☔ ❄ 🌡 🌡 🚩 ☁

Favorite Memory / Recommended Activity:

_____

_____

_____

_____

Message:

_____

_____

_____

_____

_____

_____

May we share your message?   Yes / No

Guest Name: _____ Date Stayed: _____

Traveling From: _____ Weather: ☀ ☁ ☂ ❄ 🌡 🌡 🚩 ☁

Favorite Memory / Recommended Activity:

_____

_____

_____

_____

Message:

_____

_____

_____

_____

_____

_____

May we share your message?   Yes / No

Guest Name: _____ Date Stayed: _____

Traveling From: _____ Weather: ☀ ⛅ ☂ ❄ 🌡 🌡 🚩 ☁

Favorite Memory / Recommended Activity:

_____

_____

_____

_____

Message:

_____

_____

_____

_____

_____

May we share your message?   Yes / No

Guest Name: _____ Date Stayed: _____

Traveling From: _____ Weather: ☀ ☁ ☂ ❄ 🌡 🌡 🎏 ☁

Favorite Memory / Recommended Activity:

_____

_____

_____

_____

Message:

_____

_____

_____

_____

_____

_____

May we share your message?   Yes / No

Guest Name: _____ Date Stayed: _____

Traveling From: _____ Weather: ☼ ☁ ☂ ❄ 🌡 🌡 🚩 ☁

Favorite Memory / Recommended Activity:

_____

_____

_____

_____

Message:

_____

_____

_____

_____

_____

_____

May we share your message?   Yes / No

Guest Name: _____   Date Stayed: _____

Traveling From: _____   Weather: ☀ ☁ ☂ ❄ 🌡 🌡 🚩 🌳

Favorite Memory / Recommended Activity:

_____

_____

_____

_____

Message:

_____

_____

_____

_____

_____

_____

May we share your message?   Yes / No

Guest Name: _____

Traveling From: _____

Favorite Memory / Recommended Activity:

_____

_____

_____

_____

_____

Message:

_____

_____

_____

_____

_____

_____

Date Stayed: _____

Weather: ☀ ☁ ☂ ❄ 🌡 🌡 🚩 ☁

May we share your message?   Yes / No

Guest Name: _____   Date Stayed: _____

Traveling From: _____   Weather: ☀ ☁ ☔ ❄ 🌡 🌡 🚩 🌥

Favorite Memory / Recommended Activity:

_____

_____

_____

_____

Message:

_____

_____

_____

_____

_____

_____

May we share your message?   Yes / No

Guest Name: _____   Date Stayed: _____

Traveling From: _____   Weather: ☀ ☁ ☂ ❄ 🌡 🌡 🚩 ☁

Favorite Memory / Recommended Activity:

_____

_____

_____

_____

Message:

_____

_____

_____

_____

_____

May we share your message?   Yes / No

Guest Name: _____   Date Stayed: _____

Traveling From: _____   Weather: ☀ ☁ ☂ ❄ 🌡 🌡 🚩 ☁

Favorite Memory / Recommended Activity:

_____

_____

_____

_____

_____

Message:

_____

_____

_____

_____

_____

_____

May we share your message?   Yes / No

Guest Name: _____   Date Stayed: _____

Traveling From: _____   Weather: ☀ ⛅ ☔ ❄ 🌡 🌡 🚩 ☁

Favorite Memory / Recommended Activity:

_____

_____

_____

_____

Message:

_____

_____

_____

_____

_____

_____

May we share your message?   Yes / No

Guest Name: _____ Date Stayed: _____

Traveling From: _____ Weather: ☀ ☁ ☂ ❄ 🌡 🌡 🚩 ☁

Favorite Memory / Recommended Activity:

_____
_____
_____
_____

Message:

_____
_____
_____
_____
_____
_____
_____

May we share your message?   Yes / No

Guest Name: _____   Date Stayed: _____

Traveling From: _____   Weather: ☀ ☁ ☂ ❄ 🌡 🌡 🚩 ☁

Favorite Memory / Recommended Activity:

_____

_____

_____

_____

Message:

_____

_____

_____

_____

_____

_____

May we share your message?   Yes / No

Guest Name: _____   Date Stayed: _____

Traveling From: _____   Weather: ☀ ☁ ☂ ❄ 🌡 🌡 🚩 🌳

Favorite Memory / Recommended Activity:

_____

_____

_____

_____

Message:

_____

_____

_____

_____

_____

_____

May we share your message?   Yes / No

Guest Name: _____   Date Stayed: _____

Traveling From: _____   Weather: ☀ ⛅ ☔ ❄ 🌡 🌡 🚩 ☁

Favorite Memory / Recommended Activity:

_____

_____

_____

_____

Message:

_____

_____

_____

_____

_____

_____

May we share your message?   Yes / No

Guest Name: _____   Date Stayed: _____

Traveling From: _____   Weather: ☀ ☁ ☂ ❄ 🌡 🌡 ⚑ 💨

Favorite Memory / Recommended Activity:

_____

_____

_____

_____

_____

Message:

_____

_____

_____

_____

_____

_____

May we share your message?   Yes / No

Guest Name: _____   Date Stayed: _____

Traveling From: _____   Weather: ☀ ⛅ ☔ ❄ 🌡 🌡 🎏 ☁

Favorite Memory / Recommended Activity:

_____

_____

_____

_____

_____

Message:

_____

_____

_____

_____

_____

_____

May we share your message?   Yes / No

Guest Name: _____ Date Stayed: _____

Traveling From: _____

Weather: ☀ ⛅ ☔ ❄ 🌡 🌡 🚩 ☁

Favorite Memory / Recommended Activity:

_____

_____

_____

_____

Message:

_____

_____

_____

_____

_____

_____

May we share your message?   Yes / No

Guest Name: _____   Date Stayed: _____

Traveling From: _____   Weather: ☀ ☁ ☂ ❄ 🌡 🌡 🚩 ☁

Favorite Memory / Recommended Activity:

_____

_____

_____

_____

Message:

_____

_____

_____

_____

_____

_____

May we share your message?   Yes / No

Guest Name: _____ Date Stayed: _____

Traveling From: _____ Weather: ☀ ⛅ ☂ ❄ 🌡 🌡 🚩 ☁

Favorite Memory / Recommended Activity:

_____

_____

_____

_____

Message:

_____

_____

_____

_____

_____

_____

May we share your message?   Yes / No

Guest Name: _____   Date Stayed: _____

Traveling From: _____   Weather: ☀ ⛅ ☔ ❄ 🌡 🌡 🚩 ☁

Favorite Memory / Recommended Activity:

_____

_____

_____

_____

Message:

_____

_____

_____

_____

_____

_____

May we share your message?   Yes / No

Guest Name: _____   Date Stayed: _____

Traveling From: _____   Weather: ☀ ⛅ ☔ ❄ 🌡 🌡 🚩 ☁

Favorite Memory / Recommended Activity:

_____

_____

_____

_____

Message:

_____

_____

_____

_____

_____

_____

May we share your message?   Yes / No

Guest Name: _____   Date Stayed: _____

Traveling From: _____   Weather: ☀ ⛅ ☔ ❄ 🌡 🌡 🚩 ☁

Favorite Memory / Recommended Activity:

_____

_____

_____

_____

Message:

_____

_____

_____

_____

_____

_____

May we share your message?   Yes / No

Guest Name: _____ Date Stayed: _____

Traveling From: _____ Weather: ☀ ☁ ☂ ❄ 🌡 🌡 🚩 ☁

Favorite Memory / Recommended Activity:

_____

_____

_____

_____

_____

Message:

_____

_____

_____

_____

_____

_____

May we share your message?   Yes / No

Guest Name: _____   Date Stayed: _____

Traveling From: _____   Weather: ☀ ⛅ ☔ ❄ 🌡 🌡 🚩 ☁

Favorite Memory / Recommended Activity:

_____

_____

_____

_____

Message:

_____

_____

_____

_____

_____

_____

May we share your message?   Yes / No

Guest Name: _____

Traveling From: _____

Favorite Memory / Recommended Activity:

_____

_____

_____

_____

Message:

_____

_____

_____

_____

_____

_____

_____

Date Stayed: _____

Weather: ☀ ☁ ☂ ❄ 🌡 🌡 ⚑ ☁

May we share your message?   Yes / No

Guest Name: _____   Date Stayed: _____

Traveling From: _____   Weather: ☀ ⛅ ☔ ❄ 🌡 🌡 🚩 ☁

Favorite Memory / Recommended Activity:

_____

_____

_____

_____

Message:

_____

_____

_____

_____

_____

May we share your message?   Yes / No

Guest Name: _____   Date Stayed: _____

Traveling From: _____   Weather: ☼ ☁ ☂ ❄ 🌡 🌡 🚩 ☁

Favorite Memory / Recommended Activity:

_____

_____

_____

_____

_____

Message:

_____

_____

_____

_____

_____

_____

May we share your message?   Yes / No

Guest Name: _____   Date Stayed: _____

Traveling From: _____   Weather: ☀ ☁ ☂ ❄ 🌡 🌡 🚩 ☁

Favorite Memory / Recommended Activity:

_____

_____

_____

_____

Message:

_____

_____

_____

_____

_____

May we share your message?   Yes / No

Guest Name: _____ Date Stayed: _____

Traveling From: _____ Weather: ☀ ⛅ ☔ ❄ 🌡 🌡 🚩 ☁

Favorite Memory / Recommended Activity:

_____

_____

_____

_____

Message:

_____

_____

_____

_____

_____

_____

May we share your message?   Yes / No

Guest Name: _____ Date Stayed: _____

Traveling From: _____ Weather: ☀ ⛅ ☔ ❄ 🌡 🌡 🚩 ☁

Favorite Memory / Recommended Activity:

_____

_____

_____

_____

Message:

_____

_____

_____

_____

_____

_____

May we share your message?   Yes / No

Guest Name: _____   Date Stayed: _____

Traveling From: _____   Weather: ☀ ⛅ ☂ ❄ 🌡 🌡 🚩 🌥

Favorite Memory / Recommended Activity:

_____

_____

_____

_____

_____

Message:

_____

_____

_____

_____

_____

_____

May we share your message?   Yes / No

Guest Name: _____   Date Stayed: _____

Traveling From: _____   Weather: ☀ ☁ ☂ ❄ 🌡 🌡 🚩 ☁

Favorite Memory / Recommended Activity:

_____

_____

_____

_____

_____

Message:

_____

_____

_____

_____

_____

_____

May we share your message?   Yes / No

Guest Name: _____

Date Stayed: _____

Traveling From: _____

Weather: ☀ ⛅ ☂ ❄ 🌡 🌡 🚩 ☁

Favorite Memory / Recommended Activity:

_____

_____

_____

_____

Message:

_____

_____

_____

_____

_____

_____

May we share your message?   Yes / No

Guest Name: _____ Date Stayed: _____

Traveling From: _____ Weather: ☀ ⛅ ☔ ❄ 🌡 🌡 🚩 ☁

Favorite Memory / Recommended Activity:

_____

_____

_____

_____

Message:

_____

_____

_____

_____

_____

_____

May we share your message?   Yes / No

Guest Name: _____   Date Stayed: _____

Traveling From: _____   Weather: ☀ ⛅ ☔ ❄ 🌡 🌡 🚩 ☁

Favorite Memory / Recommended Activity:

_____

_____

_____

_____

Message:

_____

_____

_____

_____

_____

_____

May we share your message?   Yes / No

Guest Name: _____ Date Stayed: _____

Traveling From: _____ Weather: ☀ ⛅ ☔ ❄ 🌡 🌡 🚩 ☁

Favorite Memory / Recommended Activity:

_____

_____

_____

_____

Message:

_____

_____

_____

_____

_____

_____

May we share your message?   Yes / No

Guest Name: _____   Date Stayed: _____

Traveling From: _____   Weather: ☀ ⛅ ☔ ❄ 🌡 🌡 🚩 ☁

Favorite Memory / Recommended Activity:

_____

_____

_____

_____

Message:

_____

_____

_____

_____

_____

May we share your message?   Yes / No

Guest Name: _____   Date Stayed: _____

Traveling From: _____   Weather: ☀ ⛅ ☂ ❄ 🌡 🌡 🚩 💨

Favorite Memory / Recommended Activity:

_____

_____

_____

_____

Message:

_____

_____

_____

_____

_____

_____

May we share your message?   Yes / No

Guest Name: _____   Date Stayed: _____

Traveling From: _____   Weather: ☀ ⛅ ☔ ❄ 🌡 🌡 🚩 ☁

Favorite Memory / Recommended Activity:

_____

_____

_____

_____

Message:

_____

_____

_____

_____

_____

_____

May we share your message?   Yes / No

Guest Name: _____   Date Stayed: _____

Traveling From: _____   Weather: ☀ ☁ ☂ ❄ 🌡 🌡 🚩 🌩

Favorite Memory / Recommended Activity:

_____

_____

_____

_____

Message:

_____

_____

_____

_____

_____

May we share your message?   Yes / No

Guest Name: _____   Date Stayed: _____

Traveling From: _____   Weather: ☀ ⛅ ☂ ❄ 🌡 🌡 🚩 ☁

Favorite Memory / Recommended Activity:

_____

_____

_____

_____

Message:

_____

_____

_____

_____

_____

May we share your message?   Yes / No

Guest Name: _____ Date Stayed: _____

Traveling From: _____ Weather: ☀ ⛅ ☔ ❄ 🌡 🌡 🚩 ☁

Favorite Memory / Recommended Activity:

_____

_____

_____

_____

_____

Message:

_____

_____

_____

_____

_____

_____

May we share your message?   Yes / No

Guest Name: _____   Date Stayed: _____

Traveling From: _____   Weather: ☀ ☁ ☂ ❄ 🌡 🌡 🚩 🌥

Favorite Memory / Recommended Activity:

_____

_____

_____

_____

_____

Message:

_____

_____

_____

_____

_____

_____

May we share your message?   Yes / No

Guest Name: _____ Date Stayed: _____

Traveling From: _____ Weather: ☀ ⛅ ☔ ❄ 🌡 🌡 🚩 💭

Favorite Memory / Recommended Activity:

_____

_____

_____

_____

Message:

_____

_____

_____

_____

_____

_____

May we share your message?   Yes / No

Guest Name: _____   Date Stayed: _____

Traveling From: _____   Weather: ☀ ⛅ ☂ ❄ 🌡 🌡 🚩 ☁

Favorite Memory / Recommended Activity:

_____

_____

_____

_____

_____

Message:

_____

_____

_____

_____

_____

_____

May we share your message?   Yes / No

Guest Name: _____ Date Stayed: _____

Traveling From: _____ Weather: ☀ ⛅ ☂ ❄ 🌡 🌡 🚩 ☁

Favorite Memory / Recommended Activity:

_____

_____

_____

_____

Message:

_____

_____

_____

_____

_____

May we share your message?   Yes   /   No

Guest Name: _____ Date Stayed: _____

Traveling From: _____ Weather: ☀ ☁ ☂ ❄ 🌡 🌡 🚩 🌩

Favorite Memory / Recommended Activity:

_____

_____

_____

_____

Message:

_____

_____

_____

_____

_____

May we share your message?   Yes / No

Guest Name: _____ Date Stayed: _____

Traveling From: _____ Weather: ☀ ☁ ☂ ❄ 🌡 🌡 🚩 🌩

Favorite Memory / Recommended Activity:

_____

_____

_____

_____

Message:

_____

_____

_____

_____

_____

May we share your message?   Yes / No

Guest Name: _____ Date Stayed: _____

Traveling From: _____ Weather: ☼ ☁ ☂ ❄ 🌡 🌡 🚩 ☁

Favorite Memory / Recommended Activity:

_____

_____

_____

_____

Message:

_____

_____

_____

_____

_____

_____

May we share your message?   Yes / No

Guest Name: _____   Date Stayed: _____

Traveling From: _____   Weather: ☼ ☁ ☂ ❄ 🌡 🌡 🚩 ☁

Favorite Memory / Recommended Activity:

_____

_____

_____

_____

_____

Message:

_____

_____

_____

_____

_____

_____

_____

May we share your message?   Yes / No

Guest Name: _____ Date Stayed: _____

Traveling From: _____ Weather: ☀ ☁ ☂ ❄ 🌡 🌡 🚩 ☁

Favorite Memory / Recommended Activity:

_____

_____

_____

_____

Message:

_____

_____

_____

_____

_____

_____

May we share your message?   Yes / No

Guest Name: _____   Date Stayed: _____

Traveling From: _____   Weather: ☀ ☁ ☂ ❄ 🌡 🌡 🚩 ☁

Favorite Memory / Recommended Activity:

_____

_____

_____

_____

Message:

_____

_____

_____

_____

_____

May we share your message?   Yes / No

Guest Name: _____   Date Stayed: _____

Traveling From: _____   Weather: ☀ ☁ ☂ ❄ 🌡 🌡 🚩 ☁

Favorite Memory / Recommended Activity:

_____

_____

_____

_____

_____

Message:

_____

_____

_____

_____

_____

_____

May we share your message?   Yes / No

Guest Name: _____   Date Stayed: _____

Traveling From: _____   Weather: ☀ ☁ ☂ ❄ 🌡 🌡 🚩 ☁

Favorite Memory / Recommended Activity:

_____

_____

_____

_____

Message:

_____

_____

_____

_____

_____

_____

May we share your message?   Yes / No

Guest Name: _____   Date Stayed: _____

Traveling From: _____   Weather: ☀ ☁ ☔ ❄ 🌡 🌡 🚩 🌳

Favorite Memory / Recommended Activity:

_____

_____

_____

_____

Message:

_____

_____

_____

_____

_____

_____

May we share your message?   Yes / No

Guest Name: _____   Date Stayed: _____

Traveling From: _____   Weather: ☀ ☁ ☔ ❄ 🌡 🌡 🚩 ☁

Favorite Memory / Recommended Activity:

_____

_____

_____

_____

Message:

_____

_____

_____

_____

_____

May we share your message?   Yes / No

Guest Name: _____   Date Stayed: _____

Traveling From: _____   Weather: ☀ ⛅ ☔ ❄ 🌡 🌡 🚩 ☁

Favorite Memory / Recommended Activity:

_____

_____

_____

_____

Message:

_____

_____

_____

_____

_____

_____

May we share your message?   Yes / No

Guest Name: _____   Date Stayed: _____

Traveling From: _____   Weather: ☀ ⛅ ☂ ❄ 🌡 🌡 🚩 ☁

Favorite Memory / Recommended Activity:

_____

_____

_____

_____

Message:

_____

_____

_____

_____

_____

May we share your message?   Yes / No

Guest Name: _____   Date Stayed: _____

Traveling From: _____   Weather: ☀ ☁ ☔ ❄ 🌡 🌡 🚩 ☁

Favorite Memory / Recommended Activity:

_____

_____

_____

_____

_____

Message:

_____

_____

_____

_____

_____

_____

May we share your message?   Yes / No

Guest Name: _____   Date Stayed: _____

Traveling From: _____   Weather: ☼ ☁ ☂ ❄ 🌡 🌡 🏴 ☁

Favorite Memory / Recommended Activity:

_____

_____

_____

_____

Message:

_____

_____

_____

_____

_____

May we share your message?   Yes / No

Guest Name: _____   Date Stayed: _____

Traveling From: _____   Weather: ☀ ⛅ ☂ ❄ 🌡 🌡 🚩 💭

Favorite Memory / Recommended Activity:

_____

_____

_____

_____

_____

Message:

_____

_____

_____

_____

_____

_____

May we share your message?   Yes / No

Guest Name: _____ Date Stayed: _____

Traveling From: _____ Weather: ☼ ☁ ☂ ❄ 🌡 🌡 🚩 ☁

Favorite Memory / Recommended Activity:

_____

_____

_____

_____

Message:

_____

_____

_____

_____

_____

_____

May we share your message?   Yes / No

Guest Name: _____ Date Stayed: _____

Traveling From: _____ Weather: ☀ ☁ ☂ ❄ 🌡 🌡 🚩 🌳

Favorite Memory / Recommended Activity:

_____

_____

_____

_____

Message:

_____

_____

_____

_____

_____

_____

May we share your message?   Yes / No

Guest Name: _____ Date Stayed: _____

Traveling From: _____ Weather: ☀ ⛅ ☂ ❄ 🌡 🌡 🚩 ☁

Favorite Memory / Recommended Activity:

_____

_____

_____

_____

Message:

_____

_____

_____

_____

_____

May we share your message?   Yes / No

Guest Name: _____ Date Stayed: _____

Traveling From: _____ Weather: ☀ ☁ ☂ ❄ 🌡 🌡 🚩 ☁

Favorite Memory / Recommended Activity:

_____

_____

_____

_____

_____

Message:

_____

_____

_____

_____

_____

_____

May we share your message?   Yes / No

Guest Name: _____ Date Stayed: _____

Traveling From: _____ Weather: ☀ ☁ ☂ ❄ 🌡 🌡 🚩 ☁

Favorite Memory / Recommended Activity:

_____

_____

_____

_____

Message:

_____

_____

_____

_____

_____

_____

May we share your message?   Yes / No

Guest Name: _____   Date Stayed: _____

Traveling From: _____   Weather: ☀ ☁ ☔ ❄ 🌡 🌡 🚩 ☁

Favorite Memory / Recommended Activity:

_____

_____

_____

_____

Message:

_____

_____

_____

_____

_____

_____

May we share your message?   Yes / No

Guest Name: _____   Date Stayed: _____

Traveling From: _____   Weather: ☼ ☁ ☂ ❄ 🌡 🌡 ⚑ ☁

Favorite Memory / Recommended Activity:

_____

_____

_____

_____

Message:

_____

_____

_____

_____

_____

May we share your message?   Yes / No

Guest Name: _____ Date Stayed: _____

Traveling From: _____ Weather: ☀ ⛅ ☔ ❄ 🌡 🌡 🚩 💭

Favorite Memory / Recommended Activity:

_____

_____

_____

_____

_____

Message:

_____

_____

_____

_____

_____

_____

May we share your message?   Yes / No

Guest Name: _____   Date Stayed: _____

Traveling From: _____   Weather: ☀ ⛅ ☂ ❄ 🌡 🌡 🚩 ☁

Favorite Memory / Recommended Activity:

_____

_____

_____

_____

Message:

_____

_____

_____

_____

_____

May we share your message?   Yes / No

Guest Name: _____   Date Stayed: _____

Traveling From: _____   Weather: ☀ ☁ ☂ ❄ 🌡 🌡 🚩 ☁

Favorite Memory / Recommended Activity:

_____

_____

_____

_____

_____

Message:

_____

_____

_____

_____

_____

_____

May we share your message?   Yes / No

Guest Name: _____   Date Stayed: _____

Traveling From: _____   Weather: ☼ ⛅ ☔ ❄ 🌡 🌡 🚩 ☁

Favorite Memory / Recommended Activity:

_____

_____

_____

_____

Message:

_____

_____

_____

_____

_____

_____

May we share your message?   Yes / No

Guest Name: _____   Date Stayed: _____

Traveling From: _____   Weather: ☀ ☁ ☂ ❄ 🌡 🌡 🚩 ☁

Favorite Memory / Recommended Activity:

_____

_____

_____

_____

_____

Message:

_____

_____

_____

_____

_____

_____

May we share your message?   Yes / No

Guest Name: _____ Date Stayed: _____

Traveling From: _____ Weather: ☀ ☁ ☂ ❄ 🌡 🌡 🚩 ☁

Favorite Memory / Recommended Activity:

_____

_____

_____

_____

Message:

_____

_____

_____

_____

_____

May we share your message?   Yes / No

Guest Name: _____ Date Stayed: _____

Traveling From: _____ Weather: ☀ ⛅ ☂ ❄ 🌡 🌡 🚩 ☁

Favorite Memory / Recommended Activity:

_____

_____

_____

_____

_____

Message:

_____

_____

_____

_____

_____

_____

May we share your message?   Yes / No

Guest Name: _____   Date Stayed: _____

Traveling From: _____   Weather: ☀ ☁ ☂ ❄ 🌡 🌡 🚩 ☁

Favorite Memory / Recommended Activity:

_____

_____

_____

_____

Message:

_____

_____

_____

_____

_____

May we share your message?   Yes / No

Guest Name: _____   Date Stayed: _____

Traveling From: _____   Weather: ☀ ☁ ☂ ❄ 🌡 🌡 🚩 🌩

Favorite Memory / Recommended Activity:

_____

_____

_____

_____

Message:

_____

_____

_____

_____

_____

_____

May we share your message?   Yes / No

Guest Name: _____ Date Stayed: _____

Traveling From: _____ Weather: ☀ ☁ ☂ ❄ 🌡 🌡 🚩 ☁

Favorite Memory / Recommended Activity:

_____

_____

_____

_____

Message:

_____

_____

_____

_____

_____

_____

May we share your message?   Yes / No

Guest Name: _____   Date Stayed: _____

Traveling From: _____   Weather: ☀ ⛅ ☔ ❄ 🌡 🌡 🚩 🐚

Favorite Memory / Recommended Activity:

_____

_____

_____

_____

Message:

_____

_____

_____

_____

_____

_____

May we share your message?   Yes / No

Guest Name: _____   Date Stayed: _____

Traveling From: _____   Weather: ☀ ⛅ ☂ ❄ 🌡 🌡 🚩 ☁

Favorite Memory / Recommended Activity:

_____

_____

_____

_____

Message:

_____

_____

_____

_____

_____

May we share your message?   Yes / No

Guest Name: _____   Date Stayed: _____

Traveling From: _____   Weather: ☀ ☁ ☂ ❄ 🌡 🌡 🚩 🌪

Favorite Memory / Recommended Activity:

_____

_____

_____

_____

_____

Message:

_____

_____

_____

_____

_____

_____

_____

May we share your message?   Yes / No

Guest Name: _____ Date Stayed: _____

Traveling From: _____ Weather: ☀ ☁ ☔ ❄ 🌡 🌡 🚩 ☁

Favorite Memory / Recommended Activity:

_____

_____

_____

_____

Message:

_____

_____

_____

_____

_____

May we share your message?   Yes / No

Guest Name: _____   Date Stayed: _____

Traveling From: _____   Weather: ☀ ⛅ ☔ ❄ 🌡 🌡 🚩 ☁

Favorite Memory / Recommended Activity:

_____

_____

_____

_____

_____

Message:

_____

_____

_____

_____

_____

_____

_____

May we share your message?   Yes / No

Guest Name: _____ Date Stayed: _____

Traveling From: _____ Weather: ☼ ☁ ☂ ❄ 🌡 🌡 🚩 ☁

Favorite Memory / Recommended Activity:

_____

_____

_____

_____

Message:

_____

_____

_____

_____

_____

May we share your message?   Yes / No

Guest Name: _____   Date Stayed: _____

Traveling From: _____   Weather: ☀ ☁ ☔ ❄ 🌡 🌡 🚩 ☁

Favorite Memory / Recommended Activity:

_____

_____

_____

_____

_____

Message:

_____

_____

_____

_____

_____

_____

_____

May we share your message?   Yes / No

Guest Name: _____   Date Stayed: _____

Traveling From: _____   Weather: ☀ ☁ ☂ ❄ 🌡 🌡 🏴 ☁

Favorite Memory / Recommended Activity:

_____

_____

_____

_____

Message:

_____

_____

_____

_____

_____

May we share your message?   Yes / No

Guest Name: _____ Date Stayed: _____

Traveling From: _____ Weather: ☀ ⛅ ☔ ❄ 🌡 🌡 🚩 ☁

Favorite Memory / Recommended Activity:

_____

_____

_____

_____

Message:

_____

_____

_____

_____

_____

_____

May we share your message?   Yes / No

Guest Name: _____   Date Stayed: _____

Traveling From: _____   Weather: ☼ ☁ ☂ ❆ 🌡 🌡 ⚑ ☁

Favorite Memory / Recommended Activity:

_____

_____

_____

_____

Message:

_____

_____

_____

_____

_____

May we share your message?   Yes / No

Guest Name: _____

Date Stayed: _____

Traveling From: _____

Weather: ☀ ⛅ ☔ ❄ 🌡 🌡 🚩 ☁

Favorite Memory / Recommended Activity:

_____

_____

_____

_____

_____

Message:

_____

_____

_____

_____

_____

_____

May we share your message?   Yes / No

Guest Name: _____ Date Stayed: _____

Traveling From: _____ Weather: ☀ ☁ ☔ ❄ 🌡 🌡 🚩 ☁

Favorite Memory / Recommended Activity:

_____

_____

_____

_____

Message:

_____

_____

_____

_____

_____

_____

May we share your message?   Yes / No

Guest Name: _____   Date Stayed: _____

Traveling From: _____   Weather: ☀ ⛅ ☂ ❄ 🌡 🌡 🚩 💨

Favorite Memory / Recommended Activity:

_____

_____

_____

_____

Message:

_____

_____

_____

_____

_____

_____

May we share your message?   Yes / No

Guest Name: _____   Date Stayed: _____

Traveling From: _____   Weather: ☀ ☁ ☂ ❄ 🌡 🌡 🚩 ☁

Favorite Memory / Recommended Activity:

_____

_____

_____

_____

Message:

_____

_____

_____

_____

_____

May we share your message?   Yes / No

Guest Name: _____   Date Stayed: _____

Traveling From: _____   Weather: ☀ ⛅ ☔ ❄ 🌡 🌡 🚩 ☁

Favorite Memory / Recommended Activity:

_____

_____

_____

_____

_____

Message:

_____

_____

_____

_____

_____

_____

May we share your message?   Yes / No

Guest Name: _____   Date Stayed: _____

Traveling From: _____   Weather: ☀ ☁ ☂ ❄ 🌡 🌡 🚩 ☁

Favorite Memory / Recommended Activity:

_____

_____

_____

_____

Message:

_____

_____

_____

_____

_____

_____

May we share your message?   Yes / No

Guest Name: _____   Date Stayed: _____

Traveling From: _____   Weather: ☀ ☁ ☂ ❄ 🌡 🌡 🚩 💨

Favorite Memory / Recommended Activity:

_____

_____

_____

_____

Message:

_____

_____

_____

_____

_____

_____

May we share your message?   Yes / No

Guest Name: _____   Date Stayed: _____

Traveling From: _____   Weather: ☀ ☁ ☂ ❄ 🌡 🌡 🚩 ☁

Favorite Memory / Recommended Activity:

_____

_____

_____

_____

Message:

_____

_____

_____

_____

_____

_____

May we share your message?   Yes / No

Guest Name: _____ Date Stayed: _____

Traveling From: _____ Weather: ☀ ☁ ☔ ❄ 🌡 🌡 🚩 ☁

Favorite Memory / Recommended Activity:

_____

_____

_____

_____

_____

Message:

_____

_____

_____

_____

_____

_____

May we share your message?   Yes / No

Guest Name: _____   Date Stayed: _____

Traveling From: _____   Weather: ☼ ⛅ ☂ ❄ 🌡 🌡 🚩 ☁

Favorite Memory / Recommended Activity:

_____

_____

_____

_____

Message:

_____

_____

_____

_____

_____

_____

May we share your message?   Yes / No

Guest Name: _____ Date Stayed: _____

Traveling From: _____ Weather: ☀ ☁ ☔ ❄ 🌡 🌡 🚩 ☁

Favorite Memory / Recommended Activity:

_____

_____

_____

_____

Message:

_____

_____

_____

_____

_____

_____

May we share your message?   Yes / No

Guest Name: _____   Date Stayed: _____

Traveling From: _____   Weather: ☀ ⛅ ☔ ❄ 🌡 🌡 🚩 ☁

Favorite Memory / Recommended Activity:

_____

_____

_____

_____

Message:

_____

_____

_____

_____

_____

May we share your message?   Yes / No

Guest Name: _____ Date Stayed: _____

Traveling From: _____ Weather: ☀ ☁ ☂ ❄ 🌡 🌡 🚩 ☁

Favorite Memory / Recommended Activity:

_____

_____

_____

_____

_____

Message:

_____

_____

_____

_____

_____

_____

May we share your message?   Yes / No

Guest Name: _____   Date Stayed: _____

Traveling From: _____   Weather: ☀ ☁ ☂ ❄ 🌡 🌡 🚩 ☁

Favorite Memory / Recommended Activity:

_____

_____

_____

_____

Message:

_____

_____

_____

_____

_____

_____

May we share your message?   Yes / No

Guest Name: _____ Date Stayed: _____

Traveling From: _____ Weather: ☀ ⛅ ☔ ❄ 🌡 🌡 🚩 ☁

Favorite Memory / Recommended Activity:

_____

_____

_____

_____

Message:

_____

_____

_____

_____

_____

_____

May we share your message?   Yes / No

Guest Name: _____ Date Stayed: _____

Traveling From: _____ Weather: ☀ ⛅ ☂ ❄ 🌡 🌡 🚩 ☁

Favorite Memory / Recommended Activity:

_____

_____

_____

_____

Message:

_____

_____

_____

_____

_____

May we share your message?   Yes / No

Guest Name: _____ Date Stayed: _____

Traveling From: _____ Weather: ☀ ☁ ☔ ❄ 🌡 🌡 🚩 ☁

Favorite Memory / Recommended Activity:

_____

_____

_____

_____

Message:

_____

_____

_____

_____

_____

_____

May we share your message?   Yes / No

Guest Name: _____ Date Stayed: _____

Traveling From: _____ Weather: ☀ ⛅ ☔ ❄ 🌡 🌡 🚩 ☁

Favorite Memory / Recommended Activity:

_____

_____

_____

_____

Message:

_____

_____

_____

_____

_____

_____

May we share your message?   Yes / No

Guest Name: _____ Date Stayed: _____

Traveling From: _____ Weather: ☀ ☁ ☂ ❄ 🌡 🌡 🚩 ☁

Favorite Memory / Recommended Activity:

_____

_____

_____

_____

Message:

_____

_____

_____

_____

_____

_____

May we share your message?   Yes / No

Made in the USA
Middletown, DE
20 April 2023

29120655R00062